# ★ American Girl®

# Parties

Photography **Nicole Hill Gerulat**

weldon**owen**

# Contents

# Let's Have a Party!

Who doesn't love an awesome party? Winter, spring, summer, or fall, you can always find a reason to throw a fabulous celebration. Whether you want to host a Valentine's Day Sweetheart Party (page 15) for your very best friends, or invite a bunch of pals to an end-of-year Winter Holiday Cookie Party (page 113), American Girl *Parties* will help you plan everything from snacks to crafts.

Each of the eight party ideas featured in this book is packed with cool tricks that are simple but so much fun. (You'll never guess how many things you can create with cookie cutters!) Make blueberry and watermelon-star skewers for a festive (and healthy) summer barbecue dessert. Or turn your favorite yogurt parfait into an ice pop dipped in granola for a seriously yummy slumber-party breakfast. Don't forget the party favors wrapped in pretty packaging—they can take your gathering from "just fine" to "the best time ever," especially if your friends get to take home what they make. Party time!

# Get creative

In these pages, you'll find tons of ideas to throw the perfect party. But think of this book as a jumping-off point that allows you to put your personal stamp on your event. Start by coming up with a theme—we give you eight different fun party plans—and then play around. Use one or all of the recipes we've gathered for that theme, then feel free to mix in some of your own favorites. Go crazy with color and don't be afraid to add a wacky dish to your menu (mint chocolate chip waffles, anyone?). Mix and match the themes or craft ideas and add your own style. Many of the recipes, like Mac & Cheese Cups (page 91) or the Ice Cream Sundae Bar (page 66), will be a hit no matter what type of bash you're hosting. Whatever your party motif—cute and cozy or big and splashy—guests will definitely remember your get-together if you add your own special flair.

# Cooking with care

When you see this symbol in the book, it means that you need an adult to help you with all or part of the recipe. Ask for help before continuing.

Adults have lots of culinary wisdom and they can help keep you safe in the kitchen. Always have an adult assist you, especially if your recipe involves high heat, sharp objects, and electric appliances. Be sure to wash your hands before you begin cooking and after touching raw meat, poultry, eggs, or seafood.

# Party prep

### PLAN YOUR THEME

What kind of party are you hosting? A birthday bash?
A movie-night sleepover? A springtime tea party? The time
of year and the weather, as well as upcoming holidays, will help
you determine the theme, location, colors, and foods to serve.

### INVITE FRIENDS

A few weeks before the party, make a guest list and send out
invitations designed with the colors and theme of your big bash.
Handcrafted notes are super cute, and your friends will love
the personal touch. Keep in mind, the bigger the party, the
more planning and prep you'll have to do.

### STAY ORGANIZED

Checklists are a great way to make sure you remember everything.
Include things like shopping for ingredients, making decorations,
setting up, and any prep you need to do before the party. Make a to-
do list for the day of your get-together so you don't forget anything.

### COOK & CRAFT AWAY

Ask friends and family to help you make table decorations, party
favors, and other crafty things a few days before the big day. Make
sure your menu includes both sweet and savory food. Prepare
dishes that can be made ahead so you have time to enjoy all the fun.

The most important thing to remember when hosting a party is to have fun!

# Sweetheart Party

On Valentine's Day, you can never have enough red, white, and pink—especially when it comes to party favors and decorations. Share the love with heart-shaped everything and sweet strawberries dipped in chocolate and sprinkles. Grilled Cheese Hearts (page 20) and Creamy Tomato Soup with Pasta Hearts (page 21) make the perfect couple. Wrap up some Raspberry Jam Heart Cookies (page 25) in pretty packaging for your friends or classmates.

### ★ Give pretty party favor bags

Fill heart-patterned cellophane bags with heart-shaped treats and tie them with pink ribbons for fun party favors.

### ★ Make your own cards

Press a pencil eraser onto a red or pink ink pad and use it to create homemade heart-art cards or party invites. A stencil makes shaping the hearts easier.

### ★ Make a heart garland

Cut out pairs of hearts and circles from patterned or colored paper and glue together each pair with a long, thin string sandwiched in between. Repeat along the string.

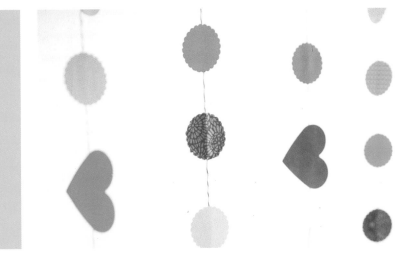

## ★ Set out festive straws

Tie a mason jar or other glass jar with a ribbon and set it next to the drinks. Fill it with patterned paper straws so everyone can help themselves.

### Be mine

*Share the love with heart-shaped treats, decorations, and favors.*

## ★ Give boxes of sweet treats

Your friends (or a secret crush) would love a festive box of goodies, like homemade cookies or granola bars. Find an array of fun holiday-themed boxes at craft stores or decorate your own with cutouts and ribbons.

# Granola Hearts with Almonds & Cranberries

These treats are not only fun for a party, they're great for packing in lunches or taking on a picnic. If you love chocolate, add ½ cup semisweet chocolate chips when you mix in the cranberries. Be sure to use unsalted nuts and seeds in this recipe.

### MAKES ABOUT 16 GRANOLA HEARTS

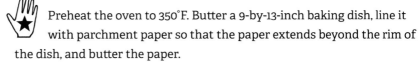

**3 tablespoons unsalted butter, plus more for greasing the baking dish**

**2 cups old-fashioned rolled oats**

**1 cup raw whole almonds, coarsely chopped**

**¼ cup raw pumpkin seeds (pepitas)**

**¼ cup raw shelled sunflower seeds**

**½ cup dried currants or raisins**

**½ cup dried cranberries**

**⅔ cup honey**

**¼ cup firmly packed light brown sugar**

**1 teaspoon vanilla extract**

**½ teaspoon salt**

Preheat the oven to 350°F. Butter a 9-by-13-inch baking dish, line it with parchment paper so that the paper extends beyond the rim of the dish, and butter the paper.

On a rimmed baking sheet, combine the oats, almonds, pumpkin seeds, and sunflower seeds. Bake, stirring the mixture once or twice, until golden, about 8 minutes. Remove the baking sheet from the oven and transfer the mixture to a large bowl. Mix in the currants and cranberries. Reduce the oven temperature to 300°F.

In a small saucepan, combine the honey, sugar, butter, vanilla, and salt. Set the pan over medium heat. Bring the mixture to a boil, stirring often, and cook until the butter is completely melted, about 30 seconds. Pour the hot honey mixture over the oat mixture and stir gently until evenly coated. Empty the mixture into the prepared baking dish and let cool slightly. Using dampened hands, press the granola into an even layer.

Bake until the granola is golden around the edges, about 20 minutes. Remove the baking dish from the oven and set it on a wire rack. Let cool for 5 minutes.

Lift the paper with the granola slab from the baking dish and place the slab on a cutting board. Using a 2½-inch metal heart-shaped cookie cutter, cut out granola hearts while the slab is still warm, pressing the mixture into the cookie cutter to mold it into a heart shape. Transfer the hearts to the wire rack and let cool completely.

# Grilled Cheese Hearts

What's not to love about crisp, buttery heart-shaped grilled cheese sandwiches? To make these sammies even more satisfying, add a slice of ham or turkey or even a few thin slices of tomato to each one. Serve with the Creamy Tomato Soup with Pasta Hearts.

MAKES 4 SANDWICHES

**8 slices whole-wheat sandwich bread**

**4 tablespoons unsalted butter, at room temperature**

**8 sandwich-size Cheddar cheese slices**

 Spread one side of each bread slice with 1½ teaspoons of butter. Turn 4 bread slices buttered side down and stack 2 cheese slices on each. Top the cheese with another slice of bread with the buttered side facing up.

Use a large heart-shaped cookie cutter—one that is as close as possible to the size of the bread slices—to cut each sandwich into a heart shape. Discard the scraps.

Set a large frying pan over medium heat. Carefully add the sandwiches and cook until golden brown on the bottom, about 3 minutes. Using a wide metal spatula, carefully flip each sandwich and cook until the second sides are golden brown, about 2 minutes.

Transfer the sandwiches to plates and serve right away.

# Creamy Tomato Soup with Pasta Hearts

Little cups of creamy tomato soup with tiny pasta hearts are perfect for a Valentine's Day party. If you can't find heart-shaped pasta, use little stars or orzo instead. And if you don't like garlic, just omit it, but don't skip the cream because it makes the soup yummy.

MAKES 4 TO 6 SERVINGS

**⅓ cup heart-shaped pasta**

**Salt and ground black pepper**

**1 teaspoon extra-virgin olive oil**

**3 tablespoons unsalted butter**

**1 small yellow onion, chopped**

**1 clove garlic, minced**

**1 (28-ounce) can diced tomatoes, with juices**

**¼ cup heavy cream**

 Fill a medium saucepan three-fourths full of water. Set the pan over high heat and bring the water to a boil. Add 1 teaspoon of salt and the pasta and cook, stirring occasionally, until the pasta is al dente (tender but still firm at the center); check the package directions for the cooking time. Drain the pasta in a colander set in the sink. Drizzle the olive oil onto the pasta and stir until evenly coated. Set the pasta aside.

Add the butter to a large saucepan. Set the pan over medium heat. When the butter has melted, add the onion and garlic and cook, stirring frequently, until the onion is soft and translucent, about 5 minutes. Add the tomatoes with their juices and bring to a boil. Reduce the heat to low and simmer, stirring occasionally, for 20 minutes. Remove the pan from the heat and let the tomato mixture cool until warm, about 30 minutes.

Transfer the tomato mixture to a blender (do this in batches if necessary). Cover and blend until the soup is smooth. Return the soup to the saucepan, stir in the cream and pasta, and bring to a gentle simmer over medium heat. Taste the soup (careful, it's hot!) and season with salt and pepper.

Ladle the soup into bowls and serve right away.

# Chocolate-Dipped Strawberries

Chocolate-dipped strawberries are scrumptious, and making them is a super-fun activity for your sweetheart party. Just line up the berries, set out a few bowls of melted chocolate along with a variety of sprinkles, and invite your friends to dip and decorate.

*MAKES ABOUT 24 STRAWBERRIES*

**STRAWBERRIES**

**1 cup semisweet chocolate chips**

**1 tablespoon vegetable shortening**

**1 pound strawberries, rinsed and dried**

**DECORATIONS**

**Multicolored sprinkles or nonpareils**

**¼ cup white chocolate chips**

To dip the strawberries, select a small saucepan and a heatproof bowl that fits snugly on top of the pan. Fill the pan one-third full of water, making sure the water doesn't touch the bottom of the bowl when the bowl is set on top of the pan. Place the saucepan over medium heat. When the water is steaming, add the chocolate chips and shortening to the bowl and place it on the saucepan. Heat, stirring occasionally with a rubber spatula, just until the mixture is melted and smooth. Remove the pan from the heat, but leave the bowl atop the pan to keep the chocolate warm until you are ready to dip.

Line a cookie sheet with parchment paper or waxed paper. Place the bowl of melted chocolate on the work surface. Working one at a time, hold each strawberry by its green stem and dip it into the melted chocolate until it is about three-fourths covered. Let excess chocolate drip back into the bowl, then place the strawberry on the prepared cookie sheet.

To decorate the berries, while the chocolate is still wet, sprinkle the berries with sprinkles, then refrigerate until set. For white chocolate stripes, refrigerate the dipped berries until set. Melt the white chocolate chips the same way that you melted the semisweet chocolate chips. Use a fork to drizzle the melted white chocolate onto the chilled berries, then refrigerate until set.

Transfer the chocolate-dipped berries to a plate and serve. (The berries are best eaten the day they're dipped, but if necessary, loosely cover them with parchment paper or waxed paper and refrigerate overnight.)

# Raspberry Jam Heart Cookies

Heart-shaped, jam-filled sandwich cookies with a dusting of powdered sugar are the perfect treat for any celebration, especially a sweetheart party. If you like, bake the cookies a day ahead, store them in an airtight container, and fill them the day of your party.

**MAKES ABOUT 16 COOKIES**

2 cups all-purpose flour

½ teaspoon salt

1 cup (2 sticks) unsalted butter, at room temperature

¾ cup powdered sugar, plus extra for dusting the cookies

2 teaspoons vanilla extract

6 tablespoons seedless raspberry jam

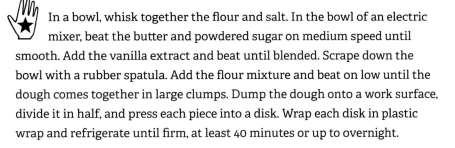

In a bowl, whisk together the flour and salt. In the bowl of an electric mixer, beat the butter and powdered sugar on medium speed until smooth. Add the vanilla extract and beat until blended. Scrape down the bowl with a rubber spatula. Add the flour mixture and beat on low until the dough comes together in large clumps. Dump the dough onto a work surface, divide it in half, and press each piece into a disk. Wrap each disk in plastic wrap and refrigerate until firm, at least 40 minutes or up to overnight.

Position 2 racks evenly in the oven and preheat the oven to 325°F. Line 2 cookie sheets with parchment paper. Sprinkle a work surface with flour. Using flour as needed, roll out one dough disk to ¼ inch thick. Using a 2½-inch heart-shaped cookie cutter, cut out as many cookies as you can. Using a 1-inch heart-shaped cookie cutter, cut out the center from half of the cookie hearts. Place the hearts on the prepared cookie sheets, spacing them evenly. Repeat with the second dough disk. Press the scraps together and repeat the process.

Bake the cookies until the edges are lightly browned, rotating the pans halfway through, 12 to 15 minutes. Let cool on a wire rack for 5 minutes, then use a metal spatula to move the cookies directly to the rack to cool completely.

Spread 1 teaspoon of raspberry jam on each heart without a cutout, leaving a ¼-inch border. Put a little powdered sugar in a sieve, dust the hearts with cut-out centers, then place on top of the jam-covered cookies. Dust the small heart cookies with powdered sugar. Serve right away or store in an airtight container at room temperature for up to 3 days.

# Garden Tea Party

This party is fit for fairies. Filled with butterflies, flowers, fancy teacups, and sparkles, it's the perfect afternoon event that you can host in the garden or at a nearby park when the weather is really nice. Use pretty, nature-inspired crafts and colors. Put real flowers (cut some fresh roses from the garden) in dainty tea cups for a sophisticated centerpiece that's as easy as 1-2-3. And oodles of bite-sized sweet treats are a must! Your guests will adore mini vanilla cupcakes topped with sparkly frosting and edible butterflies.

★ **Set out butterfly straw cutouts** Purchase butterfly-shaped cutouts that you can slip onto paper straws.

★ **Use teacups as flower vases** Gather an array of elegant, colorful teacups and use them as mini vases. Cut the stems short on your favorite big, fluffy flowers and pile them in.

★ **Get ready to party** Put on your favorite party clothes and add fresh flowers to your hair. Or weave together flower wreaths to wear as colorful crowns.

★ **Decorate with giant paper flowers** Made from multicolored tissue paper, these massive flowers add lots of bright color and pretty frills. Find them online (or make your own).

## A toast with tea

Celebrate with your friends in a pretty outdoor setting.

★ **String up butterflies** Make or purchase big colorful paper butterflies and then string them up from trees or bushes above and all around the table. They also make terrific tabletop centerpieces.

# Flower & Fruit Iced Tea

For this jewel-toned herbal refresher, use hibiscus tea, which is made from the petals of red hibiscus flowers and tastes a little like cranberry juice. You can use a hibiscus-berry tea blend instead, if you like. If you like your tea a little sweeter, add more honey.

 MAKES 4 TO 6 SERVINGS

**2½ cups water**

**3 hibiscus tea bags**

**1 tablespoon honey, plus more to taste**

**3 or 4 thin slices fresh unpeeled ginger (optional)**

**2 cups apple juice**

**Ice for serving**

**Fresh mint sprigs, for serving**

 Add the water to a small saucepan. Set the pan over medium-high heat and bring the water to a boil. Turn off the heat and add the tea bags, honey, and ginger (if using). Cover the pan and set aside for 5 minutes.

Carefully remove and discard the tea bags and ginger slices. Pour the tea into a glass pitcher. Stir in the apple juice. Taste the tea and add more honey, if you like.

Add ice to individual glasses and pour in the tea. Garnish each glass with a mint sprig and serve right away.

# Bite-Sized Chocolate Chip Scones

No tea party is complete without scones, and these dainty ones are the best because they're studded with chocolate chips. To make regular-sized scones, use a 3-inch cutter and bake them a few minutes longer. Serve the scones with butter and strawberry jam.

MAKES ABOUT 16 MINI SCONES

**2 cups all-purpose flour**

**3 tablespoons sugar**

**2½ teaspoons baking powder**

**¼ teaspoon salt**

**½ cup (1 stick) cold unsalted butter, cut into 8 chunks**

**½ cup mini semisweet chocolate chips**

**1 cup cold heavy cream**

 Preheat the oven to 400°F. Line a cookie sheet with parchment paper.

In a large bowl, whisk together the flour, sugar, baking powder, and salt. Scatter the butter chunks over the flour mixture and, using a pastry blender or 2 dinner knives, cut the butter into the dry ingredients until the mixture forms coarse crumbs about the size of peas. Stir in the chocolate chips. Pour in the cream and stir with a fork or rubber spatula just until combined.

Sprinkle a clean work surface with flour and turn the dough out onto the floured surface. Using floured hands, pat the dough into a round about ½ inch thick. Using a 1½-inch biscuit cutter, cut out as many rounds of the dough as possible. Gather up the scraps, knead briefly, and pat and cut out more rounds. Place the rounds on the prepared cookie sheet, spacing them apart evenly.

Bake until the scones are golden brown, about 10 minutes. Remove the cookie sheet from the oven and set it on a wire rack. Serve the scones warm or at room temperature.

**Sandwich toppers**
Use tissue paper pom-
pom or flower cupcake
toppers to spear your
tea sandwiches and
add a splash of color.

# Cucumber & Cream Cheese Sandwich Flowers

Nothing says "tea party" quite like these classic finger sandwiches.
They're so pretty cut into flower shapes, but you can simply slice them,
with or without the crusts, into triangles or long rectangles.

**8 slices good-quality whole-wheat or white sandwich bread**

**½ cup whipped cream cheese**

**½ small English cucumber, cut into very thin rounds**

 Spread one side of each slice of bread with 1 tablespoon of the whipped cream cheese. Top 4 of the cream cheese–covered bread slices with the cucumber slices, dividing them evenly. Place the remaining 4 bread slices on top, cream cheese side down, sandwiching the cucumber.

Use a large flower-shaped cookie cutter—one that is as close as possible to the size of the bread slices—to cut each sandwich into a flower shape. Discard the scraps. Serve right away.

# Butterfly-Shaped Pimento Cheese Sandwiches

These yummy cheesy sandwiches are super cute when transformed into butterflies, complete with edible antennae! But you can use any shape cutter you like—just be sure that it's about the same size as your slices of bread to keep the amount of waste to a minimum.

◡  **MAKES 4 SANDWICHES**  ◡

**2½ cups shredded orange-colored sharp Cheddar cheese**

**⅓ cup rinsed and drained finely chopped pimentos or roasted red peppers**

**½ cup mayonnaise**

**Pinch of sugar**

**8 slices good-quality whole-wheat or white sandwich bread**

**8 matchstick-sized pieces of carrot or celery**

 In a medium bowl, stir together the cheese, pimentos, mayonnaise, and sugar until well combined.

Spread the pimento cheese on 4 of the bread slices, dividing it evenly. Place the remaining 4 bread slices on top, sandwiching the pimento cheese. Use a large butterfly-shaped cookie cutter—one that is as close as possible to the size of the bread slices—to cut each sandwich into a butterfly shape. Discard the scraps.

Tuck 2 carrot or celery matchsticks into the pimento cheese at the top center of each butterfly to create "antennae." Serve right away.

**Edible butterflies**
Decorate cupcakes or cakes with a rainbow of butterflies made from edible wafer paper (available online).

# Mini Vanilla Cupcakes with Sparkle Frosting

Decorated with sparkling sugar or other cute sprinkles, these bite-sized cakes look like sweet treats for garden fairies. The pink icing is pretty, but you can leave it white or change it to your favorite color with a few drops of food coloring.

### MAKES 24 MINI CUPCAKES

**CUPCAKES**

1½ cups all-purpose flour

2 teaspoons
baking powder

¼ teaspoon salt

¾ cup (1½ sticks)
unsalted butter,
at room temperature

¾ cup granulated sugar

3 large eggs

2 teaspoons
vanilla extract

**FROSTING**

½ cup (1 stick)
unsalted butter,
at room temperature

3 cups powdered
sugar, sifted

Pinch of salt

1 teaspoon vanilla extract

3 drops pink
food coloring

Pink and white sparkling
sugar, for decorating

 To make the cupcakes, preheat the oven to 350°F. Line a 24-cup mini muffin pan with paper or foil liners.

In a medium bowl, whisk together the flour, baking powder, and salt. In a large bowl, using an electric mixer, beat the butter and granulated sugar on medium-high speed until light and fluffy, about 3 minutes. Add the eggs one at a time, beating well on medium speed after adding each one. Turn off the mixer and scrape down the bowl with a rubber spatula. Add the vanilla and beat until combined. Turn off the mixer. Add about one-third of the flour mixture and mix on low speed until just combined. Turn off the mixer. Add about half of the remaining flour and mix on low speed until just combined. Turn off the mixer. Add the remaining flour and mix on low speed until blended. Scrape down the bowl.

Divide the batter evenly among the muffin cups. Bake until a toothpick inserted into the center of a cupcake comes out clean, about 12 minutes. Remove the pan from the oven and set it on a wire rack. Let the cupcakes cool in the pan for 10 minutes, then transfer them to the rack. Let cool completely.

To make the frosting, in a large bowl, using an electric mixer, beat the butter, powdered sugar, and salt on medium-low speed until smooth and creamy, about 2 minutes. Turn off the mixer and scrape down the bowl with a rubber spatula. Add the vanilla and food coloring and beat until the frosting is evenly colored.

Frost the cupcakes and decorate them with the sparkling sugar. Serve.

# Springtime Celebration

When the weather warms up, it's time to celebrate. Nothing says "Spring is here!" like pretty pastels. Blue, green, and yellow look really good together, and you can use that color palette in everything from your table to your menu (mint ice cubes, anyone?). If you're throwing an Easter party, dress up hard-boiled eggs in a swirly tie-dyed pattern. Pile your table with cute bunny and bird decorations and mounds of jelly beans and candy eggs. Carry the theme into dessert with Carrot Cake Cupcakes (page 54) topped with cream cheese frosting and an edible bird's nest. And when it's time to say good-bye, seed packets are an awesome way to send your friends home with something special.

### ★ Give seed packet party favors

Spring flower and vegetable seed packets tied with twine make great party favors.

### ★ Make mint ice cubes

Add tiny mint leaves to an ice cube tray, fill it with water, and freeze to create flavorful ice cubes. They're great in all types of drinks, from sparkling water to agua fresca.

### ★ Decorate branches

For a beautiful center-piece, use wood glue to affix colorful pom-poms and bird-shaped cutouts to natural tree branches. Pots of fresh herbs are also easy ways to decorate the table.

★ **Set out bowls of colorful candy eggs**
An array of pastel-colored candy eggs, jelly beans, and Jordan almonds will add a little sweetness to your spread.

**Spring fling**
*The start of spring is the perfect time for a party.*

★ **Set a springtime table**
A pastel color palette for plates, cups, and napkins creates a fresh, springy table setting. Bowls of shredded colored paper make fun "nests" for serving tie-dyed hard-boiled eggs. Cutouts of bunnies with puffy glued-on tails add a playful touch.

# Tie-Dyed Hard-Boiled Eggs

Around Easter, dye kits for eggs are easy to find in any supermarket. At other times, you can easily purchase them online. Look for natural dyes made from herbs, vegetables, and fruits, or make your own with ½ cup boiling water, a little vinegar, and food coloring.

### ∽ MAKES 12 EGGS ∽

**1 dozen large white eggs**

**1 egg dye kit**

Place the eggs in a large saucepan (save the egg carton!) and add enough cold water to cover by about 1 inch. Cover the pan. Set the pan over high heat and bring the water to a boil. As soon as the water boils, turn off the heat and let stand, covered, for 14 minutes. Using a slotted spoon, transfer the eggs to a colander set in the sink. Discard the water in the pan. Rinse the eggs under cold running water. Fill the pan with cold water and add a few handfuls of ice cubes. Let stand until the eggs are cool, then drain again.

Prepare the dyes according to the package instructions, then pour each dye into its own bowl. Cover your work surface with newspapers, and make sure everyone wears old clothes. Line up the bowls on the work surface. Place a baking sheet with a wire rack set atop or inside of it nearby, along with the empty egg carton. Dye each egg a solid color, ideally one of the lighter colors (or leave the egg in the dye only briefly so the color stays muted). Set aside on the wire rack to dry for 15 to 30 minutes.

Using a small fork or spoon, drizzle each egg with contrasting colors. Let the eggs dry on the rack for about 30 minutes, then place in the egg carton. Refrigerate until party time.

**Egg decorating**
*Place a rack over a cookie sheet or baking dish to catch drips. Spoons work great for drizzling dye onto the eggs.*

# Turkey, Avocado & Havarti Pinwheels

These playful pinwheel-shaped sandwich bites can be made using any
type of flour tortilla, but for a fun and colorful presentation,
triple the recipe and use three different-colored tortillas.

MAKES ABOUT 16 PINWHEELS

**½ ripe avocado**

**2 (8-inch) spinach,
tomato, or whole-wheat
flour tortillas**

**2 ounces sliced
havarti cheese**

**3 to 4 ounces
sliced smoked or
roasted turkey**

 Preheat the oven to 350°F. If the avocado half contains the pit, use a
spoon to scoop out the pit and discard. Carefully peel off the skin, put
the flesh in a small bowl, and roughly mash.

Place the tortillas in a single layer on a cookie sheet. Place the cheese on
the tortillas, dividing it evenly and tearing it into smaller pieces so it
covers the tortilla evenly. Bake until the cheese melts, about 5 minutes.

Remove the cookie sheet from the oven. Transfer the tortillas to a cutting
board. Carefully arrange the turkey slices over the cheese, leaving about
1 inch uncovered on one side. Spread the mashed avocado on top of the
turkey. Starting on the turkey-covered side opposite the uncovered side,
tightly roll up each tortilla into a cylinder (the exposed melted cheese will
act as a glue to hold the cylinder together).

Trim off the ends of each cylinder. Discard (or eat!) the ends, and then
slice each cylinder crosswise into 8 pinwheels. Serve right away.

# Broccoli & Cheddar Mini Quiches

Put these adorable little quiches out on a serving platter and watch your friends and family gobble them up! You can bake these a day in advance, keep them in the fridge, and then warm them up in a 350°F oven for about 5 minutes before serving.

MAKES 14 MINI QUICHES

**1 sheet frozen all-butter pie dough, about 11 inches square, thawed**

**2 large eggs**

**2 tablespoons whole milk**

**⅓ cup finely chopped cooked broccoli**

**¼ cup finely shredded Cheddar cheese**

 Preheat the oven to 400°F. Spray 14 cups of a 24-cup mini muffin pan with nonstick cooking spray.

Lightly sprinkle a clean work surface with flour and place the dough on the floured surface. If the dough is thicker than ⅛ inch, dust your rolling pin with flour and roll out the dough to that thickness. Using a 2½-inch biscuit cutter, cut out as many rounds as possible. You need 14 rounds; if necessary, gather the scraps into a ball, roll out the dough to ⅛ inch thick, and cut out additional rounds. Make sure the dough stays very cold as you work with it; place it in the refrigerator at any time if it gets too soft and warm. Press 1 round into each greased muffin cup. The edge of the dough should be flush with the rim of the cup.

In a large liquid measuring cup, whisk together the eggs and milk. Divide the broccoli evenly among the dough-lined cups, then fill each cup with some of the egg mixture, leaving a little space at the top and dividing it evenly. (If you have leftover filling, use it to fill the unlined cups for quick frittatas.) Top with the cheese, dividing it evenly.

Bake until the quiches are puffy and golden brown, about 20 minutes. Remove the pan from the oven and set it on a wire rack. Let the quiches cool in the pan for about 5 minutes. Carefully run a small knife around the inside edge of each cup and carefully lift out each quiche. Serve warm or at room temperature.

# Honeydew-Mint Agua Fresca

Honeydew melon is the base of this refreshing drink that's sure to be a hit at your springtime party. If you love cantaloupe, just swap it out for the honeydew and follow the same instructions in this recipe. Choose a ripe, fragrant melon for the best flavor.

**MAKES 8 TO 12 SERVINGS**

**1 large, ripe honeydew melon**

**Juice of 2 lemons, plus more as needed**

**⅓ cup sugar, plus more as needed**

**½ cup fresh mint leaves**

**3 cups cold water**

**A few handfuls ice cubes**

**Fresh mint sprigs, for garnish**

 Cut the honeydew in half. Using a spoon, scrape out and discard the seeds. Scoop out the flesh and put it into a blender; discard the skin. Add the lemon juice and sugar and blend until smooth. Taste the mixture and add a little more lemon juice and sugar if you like. Pour the mixture into a large bowl and add the mint leaves. Cover and set aside in the refrigerator for at least 1 hour or up to 4 hours, to allow the flavors to blend.

When you're ready to serve, pour the melon mixture through a medium-mesh sieve set over a large pitcher. Add the water and ice and stir well. Pour the agua fresca into glasses, garnish each with a mint sprig, and serve right away.

# Carrot Cake Cupcakes

What better way to celebrate springtime than with cinnamon-spiced carrot cakes topped with gooey cream cheese frosting? Decorate with "nests" of toasted coconut and jelly beans or malted milk chocolate eggs, or sprinkle with green and orange sprinkles.

MAKES 18 CUPCAKES

## CUPCAKES

2¼ cups all-purpose flour

1½ cups firmly packed light brown sugar

1 tablespoon baking powder

1 teaspoon ground cinnamon

½ teaspoon salt

1½ cups grated carrots

¾ cup vegetable oil

4 large eggs

1½ teaspoons vanilla extract

## FROSTING

4 ounces cream cheese, at room temperature

6 tablespoons (¾ stick) unsalted butter, at room temperature

1 teaspoon vanilla extract

2 cups powdered sugar

## DECORATIONS

½ cup shredded coconut, toasted

Jelly beans or speckled malted milk chocolate eggs

 To make the cupcakes, preheat the oven to 325°F. Line 18 cups of two standard muffin pans with paper or foil liners.

In a large bowl, whisk together the flour, brown sugar, baking powder, cinnamon, and salt. In a medium bowl, combine the carrots, oil, eggs, and vanilla and stir until blended. Add the carrot mixture to the flour mixture and stir gently just until blended.

Divide the batter evenly among the prepared muffin cups, filling them only three-quarters full. Bake until a toothpick inserted into the center of a cupcake comes out clean, 16 to 18 minutes. Remove the pans from the oven and set them on a wire rack. Let the cupcakes cool in the pans for about 10 minutes, then transfer them to the rack. Let cool completely.

To make the frosting, in a large bowl, using an electric mixer, beat the cream cheese, butter, and vanilla on medium speed until smooth, about 2 minutes. Turn off the mixer and scrape down the bowl with a rubber spatula. Sift the powdered sugar into the bowl, then beat on low speed until blended.

Using a small icing spatula, frost the cupcakes. Sprinkle the icing with the toasted coconut to create "nests," then top each cupcake with three candies so that they look like "eggs." Serve.

# Shining Stars BBQ

As soon as summer rolls around, it's time to get festive. Throw an outdoor barbecue in your backyard decorated with stars, stripes, and red-white-and-blue everything. Hang easy-to-make star streamers, and cover straw bales with red blankets for a rustic touch. Fire up the grill and make yummy kebabs on a stick, and keep dessert simple and fun with a make-your-own ice cream sundae bar. Try this neat trick: use star cookie cutters to stamp out shapes from watermelon slices, then slide them on wooden skewers with blueberries. Fresh Strawberry Lemonade (page 61) will keep everyone cool while they're playing party games on the lawn.

**★ Cover straw bales for bench seats** Folding chairs are great, but straw bales are more festive! Cover them with blankets to make seats that are almost as fun as a hayride.

**★ Make shooting-star streamers** Cut out stars from colored paper, then punch two holes on either side. Thread the stars onto a colorful string to make a garland you can hang.

**★ Serve starry skewers** Use a star-shaped cookie cutter to cut sliced watermelon into stars, then thread them with blueberries onto tinseled skewers for a refreshing treat.

★ **Include fun lawn games**

Horseshoe toss, ring toss, and croquet are just some of the lively lawn games you can offer at your party for fun and entertainment.

*All-American*

Throw a big bash filled with red, white, and blue everything!

★ **Set up a sundae bar**

Nothing says "summer party" like a sundae bar. Your friends and family will line up when you bring out an array of ice creams and toppings; think chocolate sauce, whipped cream, berries, crumbled cookies, and candy.

# Fresh Strawberry Lemonade

Spruce up each glass of lemonade by adding a strawberry or lemon garnish! Using a paring knife, cut a slice of lemon halfway through or slit a whole strawberry lengthwise, keeping the top intact, then slide the lemon slice or berry onto the rim of the glass.

### MAKES ABOUT 2 QUARTS

**1½ cups fresh lemon juice**

**1¼ cups superfine sugar**

**12 strawberries, trimmed**

**6 cups cold water**

**Ice, for serving**

**Thin lemon slices, for garnish (optional)**

 Put the lemon juice and sugar in a blender and blend until the sugar is dissolved, about 1 minute. Add the strawberries and puree until very smooth, about 1 minute. Pour the mixture through a fine-mesh strainer set over a 3-quart pitcher. Stir in the water, cover, and refrigerate until well chilled.

When ready to serve, stir the lemonade and add plenty of ice and lemon slices (if using).

# Mini Corn on the Cob with Lime Butter

Nothing screams "summer" like ears of sweet, fresh corn. Cut into fun, eat-it-with-one-hand pieces, then pierce each piece with a short, sturdy wooden skewer for easy eating. Spread with zesty lime butter, corn on the cob just got better!

⌒ **MAKES 12 PIECES** ⌒

**4 ears of corn, husks and silk removed**

**4 tablespoons (½ stick) salted butter, at room temperature**

**Finely grated zest of 1 lime**

 Cut each ear of corn crosswise into thirds. In a small bowl, stir together the butter and lime zest with a fork until blended.

Fill a large pot two-thirds full of water. Set the pot over high heat and bring the water to a boil. Add the corn to the boiling water and cook until the corn kernels are tender when pierced with a fork, 5 to 7 minutes. Using tongs, carefully transfer the corn to a platter. Serve hot or at room temperature with the lime butter for spreading.

# Chicken Sausage & Veggie Kebabs

These colorful kebabs are so much fun at an outdoor party. You can use different veggies, if you like—whole button mushrooms and chunks of sweet bell peppers are also yummy. If you don't have an outdoor grill, you can cook the kebabs on a stovetop grill.

 MAKES 8 KEBABS

**4 links smoked chicken-apple sausages (about 12 ounces total and each about 6 inches long)**

**2 medium zucchini**

**24 cherry tomatoes**

**2 tablespoons extra-virgin olive oil**

**Salt and ground black pepper**

 Soak eight 10-inch bamboo skewers in water to cover for at least 30 minutes.

Cut each sausage link crosswise into 6 evenly sized pieces, for a total of 24 pieces. Trim the ends of the zucchini and cut each one in half lengthwise, then cut each half crosswise into 6 evenly sized chunks, for a total of 24 pieces.

Thread 3 sausage pieces, 3 zucchini chunks, and 3 cherry tomatoes onto each skewer, alternating them as you go. Place the kebabs in a single layer on a cookie sheet, brush them all over with the olive oil, and sprinkle each one with a pinch of salt and pepper.

Ask an adult to help you prepare a medium-hot fire in a gas or charcoal grill and clean and oil the grill grate. Alternatively, grease a large grill pan or frying pan with cooking spray.

Place the kebabs on the grill grate and cook, occasionally turning the kebabs with grill tongs, until the sausage is browned and the vegetables are tender, 10 to 15 minutes. If using a grill pan, let the pan heat for 3 minutes then carefully add the kebabs in a single layer and cook, occasionally turning, for 10 to 15 minutes. Transfer the kebabs to a platter and serve right away.

# Ice Cream Sundae Bar

This is the dessert bar of your dreams. Offer up a few different ice cream flavors and a bunch of fun toppings and listen as your friends scream for ice cream. Set the containers of ice cream in a large bowl of ice or in a small cooler to keep them from melting too fast.

⌒ **MAKES 6 SERVINGS** ⌒

**WHIPPED CREAM**

**1 cup cold heavy cream**

**1 tablespoon sugar**

**1 teaspoon vanilla extract**

**Toppings of your choice (see suggestions below)**

**¼ cup chopped toasted nuts, such as almonds, peanuts, or pecans**

**6 cherries**

**¾ cup hot fudge sauce, chocolate syrup, or caramel topping**

**2 pints vanilla and/or chocolate ice cream (or use your favorite flavors)**

 To make the whipped cream, in a bowl using an electric mixer, beat the cream, sugar, and vanilla on low speed until the cream thickens. Increase the speed to medium-high and continue to beat until the cream forms soft peaks. Be careful not to overbeat!

Set out the toppings, whipped cream, nuts, and cherries in bowls. Set out some spoons, too.

Put the hot fudge in a small saucepan. Set the pan over low heat and warm the hot fudge, stirring occasionally, just until it's smooth and pourable. Remove the pan from the heat.

Scoop the ice cream into 6 bowls, dividing it evenly. Top each serving with about 2 tablespoons of hot fudge. Allow your guests to top their sundaes however they like.

## Topping ideas

Marshmallow or caramel topping

Graham cracker squares, broken into pieces

Sliced strawberries or bananas

Raspberries

Chocolate candies

Roughly crushed chocolate crème sandwich cookies or chocolate chip cookies

Chocolate or rainbow sprinkles

# Wake Up to Waffles!

Any day is a good day for this delicious slumber party! Make breakfast the main event with oodles of waffles and toppings, cheesy scrambled eggs, and yogurt parfaits that turn breakfast into dessert. (For an unexpected morning treat, put yogurt and berries into ice-pop molds for parfait pops.) Cover the breakfast table in craft paper and use chalk to write names or draw doodles. Stick to a pink-and-blue color palette to match the berries. Writing out the morning menu on a chalkboard is a fun way to let your friends know what they're about to enjoy.

**★ Tie your spoons on** Use pretty, colorful ribbons to tie spoons around each yogurt-berry parfait cup.

**★ Make parfait pops** For a breakfast treat, freeze yogurt and berries in ice-pop molds. Once the pops are frozen, remove them from the molds, brush one side with some honey, and dip in granola.

BREAKFAST ✿ MENU ✿
★ yummy waffles
★ lots of toppings
★ scrambled eggs
★ yogurt parfaits
★ monkey bread
★ crisp bacon
★ orange juice

*fresh* berries

**★ Write your own menu** Set up a small chalkboard on your table or against the wall and write your breakfast menu on the board in chalk.

**fresh berries**

**choc chip**

### ★ Draw on the table

Cover your tabletop with craft paper, taping down the edges for a neat finish. Then put out chalk, crayons and/or markers for everyone to decorate.

*Good morning, fun!* Get creative with your after-slumber-party breakfast.

### ★ Set up a waffle bar

Waffles are a treat when served with butter and maple syrup, but they reach a whole new level with a fun array of berries, mini chocolate chips, and whipped cream to throw on top!

# Waffles with Lots of Toppings

If you're making waffles for lots of people and want to serve them all at once rather than as each one is ready, set your oven to 250°F and place a baking sheet inside. Put each waffle in the oven as it finishes cooking to keep them warm until ready to serve.

MAKES 4 TO 6 SERVINGS

2 cups all-purpose flour

1 tablespoon sugar

1 tablespoon
baking powder

¼ teaspoon salt

3 large eggs

1½ cups whole milk

6 tablespoons
(¾ stick) unsalted
butter, melted

 Preheat a waffle iron. In a medium bowl, whisk together the flour, sugar, baking powder, and salt. In a large bowl, whisk the eggs until light and frothy, then whisk in the milk and melted butter. While whisking gently, gradually add the flour mixture and mix just until combined. The batter will be lumpy.

When the waffle iron is ready, pour batter over the cooking grid. Close the lid and cook until the steam subsides and the indicator light signals that the waffle is ready, 2 to 4 minutes. Carefully open the iron, transfer the waffle to a serving plate, and serve right away with toppings. Cook the remaining batter in the same way, serving each waffle as it's ready.

## Topping ideas

Pure maple syrup

Raspberry jam or
orange marmalade

Sliced strawberries

Raspberries and/or
blueberries

Sliced pitted peaches
or nectarines

Mini chocolate chips

Sweetened
ricotta cheese

Whipped Cream
(page 66)

# Cheesy Scramble with Tomatoes & Basil

These fluffy eggs have all the ingredients of a cheese pizza: tomatoes, basil, and mozzarella. If you prefer your eggs plain, just leave out the tomatoes and basil but keep the cheese, please!

◠— MAKES 6 SERVINGS —◞

**2 teaspoons olive oil**

**1 cup cherry or grape tomatoes, halved**

**Salt and ground black pepper**

**12 large eggs**

**2 tablespoons chopped fresh basil**

**1 tablespoon unsalted butter**

**4 ounces fresh mozzarella cheese, cut into small cubes**

 Put the olive oil in a large nonstick frying pan. Set the pan over medium heat. Add the cherry tomatoes and cook, stirring occasionally, until hot and beginning to soften, about 2 minutes. Transfer to a bowl, sprinkle with a little salt and pepper, and cover to keep warm.

In a medium bowl, whisk together the eggs, 1 tablespoon of the basil, ¼ teaspoon salt, and ¼ teaspoon pepper until thoroughly blended.

Add the butter to the frying pan that you used to cook the tomatoes. Set the pan over medium-low heat. When the butter begins to foam, add the egg mixture to the pan and cook until it begins to set, about 30 seconds. Stir with a heatproof spatula, scraping the egg on the bottom and sides of the pan and folding it toward the center. Continue to stir in this way until the eggs form moist, soft curds. Stir the mozzarella and tomatoes into the eggs.

Remove the pan from the heat and let stand until the mozzarella starts to melt, about 1 minute. Sprinkle the remaining 1 tablespoon basil over the scramble and serve right away.

# Yogurt, Berry & Granola Parfaits

Making your very own granola is a ton of fun, and then using it in pretty parfaits makes it even more special. Bake up an extra batch, put it into plastic gift bags, tie the bags with ribbons, and give them to your friends as party favors.

MAKES 4 PARFAITS

**MAPLE GRANOLA**

**3 cups old-fashioned rolled oats**

**2 cups coarsely chopped almonds, pecans, and/or walnuts**

**1 cup shredded dried unsweetened coconut**

**1 cup raw shelled sunflower seeds**

**½ cup pure maple syrup, preferably Grade B**

**½ cup firmly packed light brown sugar**

**⅓ cup vegetable oil**

**1 teaspoon ground cinnamon**

**¾ teaspoon salt**

**1½ cups raisins**

**PARFAITS**

**2 cups vanilla yogurt**

**1 cup Maple Granola (or store-bought granola)**

**About 1 cup mixed berries**

 To make the maple granola, preheat the oven to 300°F. Lightly oil a roasting pan. Add the oats, almonds, coconut, and sunflower seeds to the prepared pan and mix well. In a medium bowl, whisk together the maple syrup, sugar, oil, cinnamon, and salt until the sugar dissolves. Pour the maple mixture over the oat mixture and mix with your hands until the dry ingredients are evenly moistened.

Bake, stirring every 10 minutes and making sure to move the granola from the edges of the pan to the center, until the granola is golden brown and crisp, 45 to 55 minutes. Remove the pan from the oven and set it on a wire rack. Let the granola cool completely in the pan. Stir in the raisins. (The granola can be stored in an airtight container at room temperature for up to 1 month.)

To make the parfaits, have ready 4 parfait glasses or individual bowls. Layer half of the yogurt, granola, and berries into the glasses, in that order and dividing it evenly, then layer the remaining half of the yogurt, granola, and berries. Serve right away.

# Monkey Bread with Cinnamon & Pecans

If you don't want to make your own dough, you can use one package of store-bought frozen Parker House–style rolls. Defrost the rolls, use each one as you would a dough piece, and increase the baking time to 30 minutes.

⟶ MAKES 10 TO 12 SERVINGS ⟵

## DOUGH

½ cup lukewarm (110°F) water

1 package (2½ teaspoons) active dry yeast

½ cup lukewarm (110°F) whole milk

¼ cup granulated sugar

1 teaspoon salt

1 large egg

¼ cup (½ stick) unsalted butter, melted

3 cups all-purpose flour, plus more as needed

½ cup (1 stick) plus 1 tablespoon unsalted butter, melted

½ cup chopped pecans, plus 2 tablespoons finely chopped

1 cup firmly packed light brown sugar

2½ teaspoons ground cinnamon

 To make the dough, in the bowl of a stand mixer, combine the water and yeast and let stand until foamy, about 2 minutes. Add the milk, granulated sugar, salt, and egg and whisk until blended. Stir in the melted butter and 2½ cups of the flour. Attach the dough hook to the stand mixer and mix on low speed. With the mixer running, gradually add the remaining ½ cup of flour, then increase the speed to medium and mix until a dough forms and the dough springs back when pressed with a finger, 3 to 4 minutes. The dough should be soft but not sticky; if needed, mix in more flour, 1 tablespoon at a time, to prevent sticking. Place the dough in a lightly oiled bowl and turn to coat its surface with oil. Cover with plastic wrap and let rise in a warm place until the dough has doubled in bulk, 1 to 1½ hours.

Meanwhile, using a pastry brush, coat the inside of a 10-inch Bundt pan with the 1 tablespoon of melted butter, then sprinkle the 2 tablespoons of chopped pecans in the bottom of the pan. Put the remaining ½ cup of melted butter in a shallow bowl. In another shallow bowl, mix together the brown sugar, cinnamon, and the remaining ½ cup of chopped pecans and set aside.

Lightly flour a work surface. Turn the dough out onto the floured surface and cut it into golf ball–size pieces. Working with a few pieces at a time, roll the dough balls in the melted butter to coat on all sides, then drop them into the brown sugar mixture and toss to coat.

Place the coated dough pieces in the prepared pan, arranging them in even layers. Loosely cover the pan with aluminum foil. (At this point, you can refrigerate the shaped dough in the pan overnight, covered with foil. Remove from the refrigerator and let stand at room temperature for about 1 hour before baking the bread as directed.)

Preheat the oven to 200°F for only 5 minutes, then turn off the oven. Place the pan in the warm oven and let the dough rise until doubled in bulk, 30 to 60 minutes (be sure to keep an eye on the dough so it doesn't collapse). Remove the pan from the oven and preheat the oven to 375°F.

Uncover the pan and bake until the bread is richly browned on top and a toothpick inserted into the loaf about 2 inches from the outer edge of the pan comes out clean, about 25 minutes. Remove the pan from the oven and set it on a wire rack. Let cool for 5 minutes. Ask an adult to help you place a serving plate upside down on top of the pan and, using oven mitts, hold the plate and pan together while turning them over. Carefully lift off the pan.

Let the bread cool until warm, then serve.

# Birthdays & Burgers

What could be better than a big pile of bite-sized burgers and anything-goes milkshakes on your birthday? How about a chocolate chip cookie cake? This is the kind of party where you can go crazy with crafts. Fun paper cones with wacky patterns are perfect for serving Baked Sweet Potato Fries (page 88). Scatter rainbow-colored confetti over the tables, and mix and match bowls of all shapes and sizes to hold a variety of milkshake toppings. White Chocolate–Dipped Pretzels (page 96) are a festive favor idea—top them with colorful sprinkles that match your party theme.

**★ Set up a space to showcase gifts**
Designate a small table or a shelf for gifts, then decorate with colorful streamers or crafts.

**★ Top your milkshakes**
Set out bowls of rainbow sprinkles and colored sugars and invite guests to add some pizzazz to their milkshakes.

**★ Decorate with color**
For a fun, happy atmosphere, decorate with bright, whimsical shapes and colors. Contrasting hues help create a festive look and feel.

★ **Hand out party hats**
To get your guests into the celebratory spirit, hand out fun, colorful party hats. Let everyone choose their favorite color.

*Birthday fun*
*A birthday is the ultimate reason to party, so make sure it's memorable!*

★ **Choose a pretty cake stand**
Nearly any kind of cake can look festive and party-ready when placed on a colorful cake stand and surrounded by pretty decorations. Top your cake with sparkly cupcake toppers to add some fun.

# Build-Your-Own Turkey Sliders

Set out all of your toppings and condiments before you start cooking the burgers. That way, when the sizzling sliders are ready, your guests can build them right away, while the patties are still warm and juicy and the buns are nice and toasty.

*MAKES 16 SLIDERS*

**FOR SERVING**

**Ketchup, mustard, and mayonnaise**

**Sliced pickles**

**Sliced tomatoes**

**Small romaine lettuce leaves**

**Sliced avocado**

**SLIDERS**

**2 pounds ground dark-meat turkey**

**2 tablespoons ketchup**

**1 tablespoon Dijon mustard**

**1 teaspoon salt**

**¼ teaspoon ground black pepper**

**16 small Cheddar cheese slices**

**16 slider buns or dinner rolls, split**

 Set out bowls of ketchup, mustard, and mayonnaise and plates of sliced pickles, sliced tomato, lettuce leaves, and sliced avocado.

To make the sliders, in a large bowl, combine the turkey, ketchup, mustard, salt, and pepper. Using clean hands, mix until the meat and seasonings are well combined, then divide the mixture into 16 equal pieces. Form each piece into a patty, making it a little bit larger than the diameter of your buns (the patties will shrink slightly when they cook). Place in a single layer on a baking sheet. Wash your hands with warm, soapy water.

Coat a large grill pan or frying pan with nonstick cooking spray. Ask an adult to help you set the pan over medium-high heat and let the pan heat for about 2 minutes. Carefully place the patties in the pan, adding only as many as will comfortably fit in a single layer; you may need to cook the patties in 2 batches. Cook until browned on the bottoms, about 5 minutes. Using a metal spatula, flip over the patties, place a slice of cheese on each one, and continue to cook until the cheese is melted and the meat at the center of the thickest patty is no longer pink, about 5 minutes longer. Using the spatula, transfer the patties to a warm platter.

Working in batches, place the buns cut side down in the pan and cook until lightly browned, 1 to 4 minutes. Transfer to a separate platter.

Serve the patties and buns along with the toppings of your choice and invite your guests to build their own sliders.

# Baked Sweet Potato Fries

A burger party just isn't complete without french fries, but deep-frying is a lot of work. With this recipe, you can make things easier—and a little healthier—by baking up yummy, crispy sweet potato fries. Serve these with ketchup or ranch dressing.

⌒ **MAKES 4 SERVINGS** ⌒

**2 pounds orange-fleshed sweet potatoes, peeled**

**3 tablespoons olive oil**

**Salt**

 Preheat the oven to 425°F. Cut the sweet potatoes lengthwise into ¼-inch-thick planks, then cut the planks lengthwise into ¼-inch sticks.

On a large rimmed baking sheet, toss the sweet potatoes with the olive oil and a large pinch of salt until evenly coated. Spread the potatoes in a single layer.

Bake until the sweet potatoes are tender and golden brown, 20 to 25 minutes. Remove the baking sheet from the oven. Sprinkle the fries with a little more salt and serve right away.

**Fun paper cones**
Roll colorful patterned paper into a cone shape and tape it to hold it in place, then fill it with fries!

# Mac & Cheese Cups

Creamy macaroni and cheese will get lots of cheers from your guests, especially when baked in cute individual cups. Use ½-cup ramekins or custard cups, or even small ovenproof teacups. For extra yumminess, top each with crumbled bacon.

MAKES 6 SERVINGS

**Salt**

**8 ounces dried elbow macaroni pasta**

**2 tablespoons unsalted butter**

**2 tablespoons all-purpose flour**

**1 cup whole milk**

**½ cup half-and-half**

**2 cups shredded white Cheddar cheese**

**2 tablespoons grated Parmesan cheese**

**2 tablespoons panko bread crumbs**

**2 tablespoons crumbled cooked bacon (optional)**

Preheat the oven to 425°F. Fill a large saucepan three-fourths full of water. Set the pan over high heat and bring the water to a boil. Add 1 tablespoon of salt and the pasta and cook, stirring occasionally, until almost tender (the noodle should still be very firm at the center), about 2 minutes less cooking time than the package instructs. Drain the pasta in a colander set in the sink, then transfer it to a large bowl.

Add the butter to the same saucepan. Set the pan over medium-high heat. When the butter is melted, add the flour and cook, stirring well, until well combined, 1 to 3 minutes. Slowly whisk in the milk and half-and-half, then bring the mixture to a boil while whisking constantly. Cook, whisking frequently to smooth out any lumps, until the mixture has thickened, 4 to 5 minutes. Remove the pan from the heat. Add a pinch of salt and two-thirds of the Cheddar cheese and whisk until smooth.

Pour the cheese sauce over the pasta and stir until well combined. Divide the pasta mixture among six ½-cup ramekins. Top evenly with the remaining Cheddar cheese and the Parmesan, then sprinkle with the panko and bacon (if using). Place the ramekins on a rimmed baking sheet.

Bake until the tops are lightly browned and the cheese sauce is bubbly, 12 to 16 minutes. Remove the baking sheet from the oven. Let cool for about 5 minutes, then serve.

# Make-Your-Own Milkshakes

A tall frothy milkshake is the ideal companion to a burger, and with this recipe, you and your friends can blend up your favorite flavors to wash down your sliders. Don't forget to top each milkshake with a big dollop of whipped cream!

*MAKES 4 TO 6 MILKSHAKES*

**1 cup whole milk, plus more as needed**

**2 teaspoons vanilla extract**

**1 quart vanilla ice cream**

**Whipped Cream (page 66)**

**Chocolate or rainbow sprinkles (optional)**

 Put the milk in a blender, followed by the vanilla and then scoops of the ice cream. Cover and blend until smooth, adding more milk as needed to achieve the consistency you desire.

Pour the milkshake into tall chilled glasses, dividing it evenly. Top each with a dollop of whipped cream, add sprinkles (if using), and serve right away.

## Flavor variations

**Strawberry:** *Add ⅓ cup strawberry preserves and 2 cups sliced strawberries along with the ice cream and blend as directed.*

**Chocolate:** *Add ⅓ cup chocolate syrup along with the ice cream and blend as directed.*

**Vanilla Malted:** *Add ¼ cup malted milk powder along with the vanilla and blend as directed.*

**Banana:** *Add 3 frozen peeled and sliced bananas along with the ice cream and blend as directed.*

**Choco-Banana:** *Add ⅓ cup chocolate syrup and 2 frozen peeled and sliced bananas along with the ice cream and blend as directed.*

# Chocolate Chip Cookie Birthday Cake

A birthday party just isn't a birthday party without a festive cake. This cake is like a giant chocolate chip cookie, so what's not to love? Decorate the cake as suggested, or double the recipe to make two cakes and layer with your favorite chocolate frosting.

### MAKES 8 TO 10 SERVINGS

2 cups all-purpose flour

2 teaspoons
baking powder

½ teaspoon salt

¾ cup (1½ sticks)
unsalted butter, at
room temperature,
plus more for
greasing the pan

1⅓ cups firmly packed
light brown sugar

2 large eggs

1½ teaspoons
vanilla extract

1½ cups semisweet
chocolate chips

Whipped Cream
(page 66)

11 strawberries,
hulled

 Preheat the oven to 350°F. Grease a 9-inch round cake pan with butter. Sprinkle some flour in the pan and shake and tilt the pan to evenly coat the bottom and sides. Turn the pan upside down and tap out the excess flour.

In a small bowl, whisk together the flour, baking powder, and salt. In a large bowl, using an electric mixer, beat the butter and sugar on medium speed until creamy, about 3 minutes. Turn off the mixer and scrape down the bowl with a rubber spatula. Add the eggs, one at a time, beating on medium speed until blended. Add the vanilla and beat until blended. Turn off the mixer. Add the flour mixture and mix on low speed just until blended. Stir in the chocolate chips. The dough will be very thick. Scrape the dough into the prepared pan and spread it into an even layer.

Bake until a toothpick inserted into the center of the cake comes out with a few crumbs clinging to it, 40–45 minutes. Remove the pan from the oven and set it on a wire rack. Let cool for 30 minutes. Run a paring knife around the inside edge of the pan to loosen the cake. Ask an adult to help you place the rack upside down on top of the pan and, holding the two together, turn them over. Lift off the pan. Place a serving plate upside down on top of the cake and invert the cake right side up onto the plate. Let the cake cool completely.

Mound the whipped cream on top of the cake and spread it evenly over the top. Place 10 strawberries, pointed sides up, around the edge and 1 in the center. Serve right away.

# White Chocolate–Dipped Pretzels

White chocolate–dipped pretzels with colorful sprinkles make great party gifts for guests. They're also just super-yummy to eat! If you prefer milk chocolate or dark chocolate, you can use it instead of the white chocolate.

MAKES 36 TO 40 MINI PRETZELS

**4 ounces good-quality white chocolate, chopped**

**36 to 40 mini pretzels**

**Rainbow sprinkles or colored sparkling sugar, for decorating**

 Line a cookie sheet with wax or parchment paper.

Select a saucepan and a heatproof bowl that fits snugly on top of the pan. Put the chocolate in the bowl. Fill the pan about one-third full of water, making sure the water doesn't touch the bottom of the bowl when the bowl is set on top of the pan. Place the saucepan over medium-low heat. When the water is steaming, place the bowl on top of the saucepan. Heat the chocolate, stirring occasionally with a rubber spatula, until melted and smooth. Don't let the chocolate get too hot, and use pot holders or oven mitts if you need to touch the bowl. Remove the bowl from the saucepan and let the chocolate cool slightly.

Using your fingers, hold a pretzel in the center and carefully dip it into the melted chocolate, completely covering one side. Place the pretzel chocolate-side-up on the prepared cookie sheet and immediately sprinkle it with sprinkles (the chocolate needs to be wet when you decorate so that the sprinkles will stick). Repeat with the remaining pretzels. If the chocolate in the bowl starts to harden, place it over the hot water in the saucepan and stir until it's once again melted and smooth.

Refrigerate the pretzels until the chocolate sets, about 15 minutes. Serve.

# Spooky & Berry Delicious

This Halloween, you can throw the most fun—and scariest—party on the block. Your guests will scream with delight when they see all the yummy Halloween-themed goodies, both savory and sweet, that you've cooked up in your cauldron to get them in the spirit. Get your scare on with blood-red smoothies, cheesy "bone" twists, and hot dog "mummies." We go batty for easy-peasy masks, straws, and smoothie wrappers made from black craft paper. And send them running home with treats swallowed up by googly-eyed monster bags.

**★ Make bat sleeves**
Cut out bat shapes from black paper, then glue them to coffee cup sleeves that fit snugly on your glasses. Use with smoothies or other party drinks.

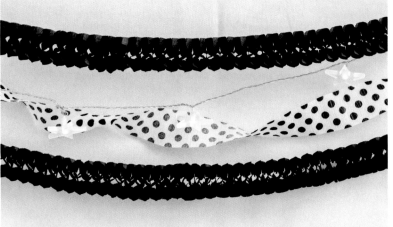

**★ Decorate with streamers and string lights** Create a festive party atmosphere with black, white, and orange streamers and lights.

**★ Give festive bags of candy** Load up small cellophane bags with your favorite candies and tie them with ribbons in Halloween colors.

★ **Draw scary faces on balloons** Use a permanent black marker to draw spooky faces on a variety of helium-filled balloons. Tie them with colorful ribbons or string.

*Boo!*
*Get in the spooky spirit with some of these fun craft ideas.*

★ **Make monster treat bags**
Fold down the tops of colored lunch bags (decorated with patterns, if you like). Glue googly eyes onto each flap, cut out and glue on white "teeth," and clip on two mini clothespins to make silly horns.

# Spooky Berry Smoothies

These tangy blood-red smoothies are a sweet treat for a ghoulish get-together. Serve them in tall glasses with festive straws. If you like, swap out frozen raspberries for the strawberries, or strawberry sorbet for the raspberry sorbet.

**1-pound package frozen strawberries**

**2½ cups cherry, cranberry, or cran-raspberry juice, plus more as needed**

**1 cup raspberry sorbet**

**12 ice cubes, plus more as needed**

 Add all of the ingredients to a blender and blend for 1 to 2 minutes, until smooth, adding more juice or ice as needed to create the consistency you like. You may need to do this in batches, in which case, put half of the ingredients in your blender and proceed as directed, then repeat with the remaining ingredients.

Divide the smoothies between glasses and serve right away.

# Cheese Twist "Bones"

These airy, cheesy treats baked into bone shapes are as tasty as they are fun to eat. For the best flavor, look for all-butter puff pastry in the freezer case of a well-stocked market. If you want plain cheese straws, don't cut the ends and leave them as twists.

⌐ **MAKES ABOUT 18 "BONES"** ◞

**1 (14-ounce) package frozen all-butter puff pastry, thawed overnight in the refrigerator**

**1 large egg, beaten with 1 teaspoon water**

**½ cup shredded Italian cheese blend or Parmesan**

Preheat the oven to 400°F. Line 2 cookie sheets with parchment paper. Sprinkle a work surface with flour. Unfold the puff pastry on the floured surface with a long side near you. It should measure 11 by 14 inches and be ⅛ inch thick. If not, use a rolling pin to roll it to those dimensions.

Brush the pastry sheet with egg wash, then sprinkle the cheese mixture evenly on top. Fold the top third of the pastry down and press gently to seal. Brush the uncovered pastry with egg wash, then fold the bottom third of the pastry up over the egg-washed area. Press to seal.

Using a rolling pin, roll out the pastry into a rectangle measuring about 20 inches long and 5 inches wide. Trim the short edges of the rectangle, then cut the pastry crosswise into 1-inch strips; you should have about 18 strips. Brush the strips with egg wash. Using a paring knife, slit the end of each strip, cutting 1 inch into the pastry and centering the cut on the strip.

Lift up a strip, holding one end in each hand, and turn the ends in the opposite direction to make a twist. Place on one of the prepared cookie sheets, pressing it down so that it stays in place, and pull the slit ends of the strip wide apart so that the shape resembles a bone. Repeat with the remaining strips, placing about 9 "bones" on each cookie sheet and spacing them evenly apart.

Place 1 cookie sheet in the refrigerator and the second cookie sheet in the oven. Bake until the "bones" are nicely browned, about 15 minutes. Remove the cookie sheet from the oven and set it on a wire rack. Bake the second cookie sheet of "bones" in the same way. Let cool to room temperature and serve.

# Veggie Hot Dog "Mummies"

Similar to pigs in blankets, these hot dogs are "mummified" in a homemade biscuit dough that bakes up light and fluffy. Dots of ketchup or mustard look like scary mummy eyes. If you prefer, use chicken hot dogs in place of the veggie dogs.

*MAKES 6 SERVINGS*

**BISCUIT DOUGH**

**2 cups all-purpose flour, plus more for sprinkling**

**1 tablespoon baking powder**

**¾ teaspoon salt**

**6 tablespoons (¾ stick) cold unsalted butter, cut into small chunks**

**1 cup whole milk or buttermilk**

**6 tablespoons shredded Cheddar cheese**

**6 veggie or chicken hot dogs, each 6 inches long**

**Ketchup and mustard, for serving**

Preheat the oven to 450°F. Line a baking sheet with parchment paper. To make the biscuit dough, in a large bowl, whisk together the flour, baking powder, and salt. Scatter the butter chunks over the flour mixture and, using a pastry blender or 2 dinner knives, cut the butter into the dry ingredients until the mixture looks like coarse crumbs, with small pieces of butter still visible. Pour the milk over the mixture and stir gently with a wooden spoon until clumps form.

Sprinkle a clean work surface with flour. Dump the dough onto the floured surface and knead it a few times until smooth. Using a rolling pin, roll out the dough to a 10-by-15-inch rectangle about ⅓ inch thick, sprinkling flour on the dough as needed to prevent sticking. Cut the rectangle into six 5-inch squares. Sprinkle each dough square with 1 tablespoon of the cheese. Place a hot dog diagonally in the center of each dough square. Lift one uncovered corner of the square up and over the hot dog and press it gently in place. Brush the top of the dough point on the hot dog with water, then lift the opposite corner up and over, wrapping it snugly around the hot dog and the first dough layer, and press gently to help it adhere. Repeat with the remaining hot dogs and dough squares. Place the wrapped hot dogs, seam side up and spaced evenly apart, on the prepared baking sheet.

Bake until the dough is golden brown, 10 to 13 minutes. Remove the baking sheet from the oven and set it on a wire rack. Let cool for a few minutes, then dot two "eyes" on each hot dog with ketchup or mustard. Serve warm.

# Chocolate-Orange Checkerboard Cookies

These cute orange and dark brown checkerboard cookies are the colors of Halloween. Prepare the dough logs a day in advance to get a head start. The logs also freeze well in a plastic freezer bag. Just thaw them overnight in the fridge before slicing and baking.

MAKES ABOUT 30 COOKIES

1 cup all-purpose flour

¼ teaspoon
baking powder

⅛ teaspoon salt

½ cup (1 stick)
unsalted butter,
at room temperature

½ cup sugar

1 large egg, separated

1 teaspoon
vanilla extract

1 teaspoon grated
orange zest

A few drops orange
food coloring

1 ounce semisweet
chocolate, melted

2 teaspoons
cocoa powder

 In a bowl, whisk together the flour, baking powder, and salt. In the bowl of an electric mixer, beat the butter and sugar on medium speed until creamy, about 2 minutes. Add the egg yolk and vanilla and beat until combined. Add the flour mixture and mix on low speed until blended and the dough is smooth. Scrape down the bowl and divide the dough in half. Put one half in a separate bowl and stir in the zest and food coloring. Add the melted chocolate and cocoa to the dough remaining in the bowl and mix on low speed until well blended. Form each portion of dough into a square, wrap separately in plastic wrap, and refrigerate until firm, about 45 minutes.

In a bowl, beat the egg white until foamy. Remove the dough from the refrigerator and cut each into 4 strips. Roll each strip into a ½-inch-thick rope, flouring your hands to prevent sticking. Gently press each rope against the work surface to create squared-off sides. Brush the ropes lightly with egg white. Press a chocolate and orange rope together, then top with 2 ropes, positioning chocolate on the orange and orange on the chocolate. Press to seal. Trim the ends and wrap in plastic wrap. Repeat with the remaining 4 dough ropes. Refrigerate the logs until firm, at least 1 hour or up to overnight.

Position 2 racks evenly in the oven and preheat the oven to 350°F. Line 2 cookie sheets with parchment paper. Cut the dough crosswise into slices ¼ inch thick, then place on the prepared cookie sheets. Bake the cookies until the edges are golden, 8 to 12 minutes. Let cool on the pan on a wire rack for 5 minutes, then use a spatula to move the cookies directly to the rack. Serve.

# Caramel-Dipped Apple Wedges

Whole apples covered in caramel look great, but they're difficult to eat. These caramel-dipped apple slices are perfect for a party, and you can enjoy them in just a couple of delicious bites. The pecans are optional, but they add lots of yummy flavor and texture.

◦— MAKES 16 PIECES —◦

**¾ cup chopped pecans or almonds (optional)**

**1 (11-ounce) bag soft caramel candies**

**2 tablespoons water**

**4 apples, quartered and cored**

If using the pecans or almonds, preheat the oven to 350°F. Spread the nuts in a single layer on a small cookie sheet. Toast the nuts in the oven, stirring once, until golden and fragrant, about 8 minutes. Remove the baking sheet from the oven and transfer the nuts to a shallow bowl. Set aside.

Line a baking sheet with waxed paper. Unwrap the caramels, place them in a small saucepan, and add the water. Place the pan over medium heat and cook, stirring occasionally, until the caramels have melted and the mixture is smooth, 5 to 7 minutes. Reduce the heat to low.

Hold an apple wedge by one end and dip it in the caramel so that half of it is coated. Let the excess caramel drip back into the pan. If using the nuts, roll the caramel-coated part of the apple in the nuts, pressing gently to help them adhere. Place on the prepared baking sheet. Repeat with the remaining apple wedges. Let stand until the caramel sets, about 10 minutes. Serve, or wrap the apple wedges individually in waxed paper and refrigerate for up to 1 day. Bring to room temperature before serving.

# Winter Holiday Cookie Party

Wintry days are the best days to invite friends over for a cookie extravaganza. This silver, white, and blue color scheme is both sweet and sophisticated—plus a touch of sparkle makes it party-rific. Try this trick: cut snowflakes from white coffee filters and string them together to make a pretty garland. Super-cute cookie cutters and big mugs of hot cocoa filled to the rim with marshmallows are a must! And definitely sneak candy canes into as many baked treats as you can, like the ooey-gooey Peppermint Brownie Bites (page 120). Pretty cookie boxes filled with home-baked goodies and tied with shiny ribbons are the ultimate party favors or gifts.

★ **Serve hot drinks**
Hot chocolate with mini marshmallows or steaming cups of tea go great with cookies.

★ **Make snowflakes**
Fold a white coffee filter in half, then repeat folding 3 times. Cut shapes from the 2 straight sides, then open to reveal a snowflake. String them up with twine to create a garland.

★ **Have boxes and bows for cookies** Gather an array of festive boxes and colorful holiday ribbons and bows so you can create pretty cookie packages for your friends.

★ **Create a forest of paper cone trees** Form white card-stock paper into cone shapes, then wrap and glue decorative paper around each cone. Set them up together like a forest!

*Winter sparkle*
Warm up cold days by creating a cookie wonderland!

★ **Mix and match cookie shapes** Ask your friends to bring their favorite cookie cutters. Then, use the gingerbread dough (see page 117) to cut out a variety of shapes for baking and decorating.

# Gingerbread Family Cookies

Choose a variety of different-shaped cutters for these cookies. Ice them with a piping cone, then decorate with small candies, currants or raisins, mini chocolate chips, and colorful sprinkles and sparkling sugar. After decorating, let the icing dry until it sets.

⌒ **MAKES ABOUT 24 COOKIES** ⌒

**GINGERBREAD COOKIES**

2¾ cups all-purpose flour

2½ teaspoons baking powder

1 tablespoon ground ginger

1½ teaspoons ground cinnamon

½ teaspoon ground nutmeg

¼ teaspoon salt

½ cup (1 stick) unsalted butter, at room temperature

⅔ cup firmly packed light brown sugar

1 teaspoon vanilla extract

1 large egg

⅓ cup dark molasses

**ICING**

2 cups powdered sugar

2 tablespoons plus 2 teaspoons warm water

1 tablespoon light corn syrup

 To make the gingerbread cookies, in a bowl, whisk together the flour, baking powder, ginger, cinnamon, nutmeg, and salt. In the bowl of an electric mixer, beat the butter and brown sugar on medium speed until creamy, about 3 minutes. Add the vanilla, egg, and molasses and beat until blended. Scrape down the bowl with a rubber spatula. Add the flour mixture and mix on low speed until the dough looks like moist pebbles, about 1 minute. Dump the dough onto a clean work surface, press it together, then divide it in half. Press each mound into a disk, wrap in plastic wrap, and refrigerate for 1 hour.

Position 2 racks evenly in the oven and preheat to 350°F. Line 2 cookie sheets with parchment paper. Sprinkle a work surface with flour. Unwrap 1 chilled dough disk, sprinkle with flour, and roll out the dough to ¼ inch thick. Use more flour as needed so the dough doesn't stick. Cut shapes out of the dough with cookie cutters and set on the prepared cookie sheet. Repeat with the remaining dough, pressing the dough scraps together.

Bake until lightly browned around the edges, rotating the cookie sheets halfway through, 10 to 12 minutes. Let cool on the cookie sheet on a wire rack for about 15 minutes, then use a metal spatula to move the cookies directly to the rack. While the cookies are cooling, bake any remaining cookies the same way. Let the cookies cool completely.

To make the icing, in a bowl, whisk together the powdered sugar, water, and corn syrup until smooth. Decorate the cookies with the icing (see Note above for ideas). Let the icing set for about 30 minutes, then serve.

# Peppermint Brownie Bites

Brownies are great for several reasons: they're super easy to make, they're endlessly versatile, and everyone loves them. This version, which is made with two kinds of mint candies, is perfect for the holidays.

*MAKES 16 BROWNIE BITES*

¾ cup (1½ sticks) unsalted butter, cut into chunks

6 ounces unsweetened chocolate, coarsely chopped

5 or 6 regular-size candy canes, unwrapped

3 large eggs

1½ cups sugar

2 teaspoons vanilla extract

¼ teaspoon salt

1 cup all-purpose flour

16 small chocolate-covered peppermint patty candies, unwrapped

Preheat the oven to 350°F. Spray an 8-inch square baking dish with nonstick cooking spray (you can use a 9-inch square baking dish instead, but the brownies will be thinner).

In a small saucepan, combine the butter and chocolate. Place the pan over medium-low heat and heat the mixture, stirring often, until melted and smooth. Remove from the heat and let cool slightly.

While the chocolate mixture cools, put the candy canes in a large zipper-lock plastic bag. Using a rolling pin, lightly crush them into small chunks. You should have ⅓ to ½ cup of crushed candy canes.

In a large bowl, whisk together the eggs, sugar, vanilla, and salt until blended. Add the chocolate mixture and whisk until blended. Add the flour and whisk slowly just until no lumps remain.

Pour about two-thirds of the batter into the prepared pan and spread it evenly with a rubber spatula. Top with the peppermint patty candies in a single layer. Dollop the remaining brownie batter over the top, gently smoothing into an even layer. Sprinkle the crushed candy canes on top of the batter.

Bake until a toothpick inserted into the center of the brownies comes out with only moist crumbs attached, about 40 minutes. (Be careful not to overbake.) Remove the baking dish from the oven and set it on a wire rack. Let cool completely. Cut the brownies into 16 squares and serve.

**Choco-rama**
*If you like plain brownies, just leave out the 2 types of peppermint candies and bake as directed.*

# Chocolate-Peanut Butter Drop Cookies

The combination of chocolate and peanut butter is so outrageously yummy in these chewy cookies. You can use either smooth or crunchy peanut butter, depending on your preference. Serve them with tall glasses of cold milk.

MAKES ABOUT 25 COOKIES

1¼ cups peanut butter, at room temperature

⅔ cup firmly packed light brown sugar

1 large egg

1 teaspoon vanilla extract

½ cup all-purpose flour

About 25 chocolate drop candies, unwrapped

 Preheat the oven to 350°F. Line a cookie sheet with parchment paper.

In a large bowl, using an electric mixer, beat the peanut butter and brown sugar on medium speed until blended, about 30 seconds. Turn off the mixer and scrape down the bowl with a rubber spatula. Add the egg and vanilla and beat on medium speed until blended. Turn off the mixer. Add the flour and mix on low speed just until blended.

Scoop up a rounded tablespoonful of dough. Scrape the dough off the spoon into the palm of your other hand and roll the dough into a ball. Place the ball on the prepared baking sheet. Repeat with the remaining dough, spacing the balls about 1 inch apart on the baking sheet.

Bake for 10 to 12 minutes, until the cookies are puffed and appear dry on top. Remove the baking sheet from the oven and set it on a wire rack. Immediately place a chocolate candy, tip pointing up, in the center of each cookie and gently press it down to sink the candy into the cookie. Let cool for 10 minutes, then use a metal spatula to move the cookies directly to the rack. Let cool completely and serve.

# Kitchen Sink Cookies

As you might guess from their name, these cookies have it all. Chock-full of oats, chocolate chips, shredded coconut, and toasty almonds, they offer something for everyone. For crispier cookies, press the mounds flat and bake for an additional 2 minutes.

MAKES ABOUT 3½ DOZEN COOKIES

**1 cup slivered almonds**

**1½ cups all-purpose flour**

**½ teaspoon baking powder**

**½ teaspoon baking soda**

**¼ teaspoon salt**

**1 cup (2 sticks) unsalted butter, at room temperature**

**¾ cup firmly packed light brown sugar**

**½ cup granulated sugar**

**2 large eggs**

**1½ teaspoons vanilla extract**

**2 cups old-fashioned rolled oats**

**1 cup sweetened shredded coconut**

**1 (12-ounce) bag semisweet or bittersweet chocolate chips**

Position 2 racks evenly in the oven and preheat to 350°F. Spread the almonds on a rimmed baking sheet and toast in the oven, stirring once or twice, until lightly golden, about 8 minutes. Remove the baking sheet from the oven. Let the nuts cool completely.

Increase the oven temperature to 375°F. Line 2 cookie sheets with parchment. In a medium bowl, whisk together the flour, baking powder, baking soda, and salt. In a large bowl, using an electric mixer, beat the butter, brown sugar, and granulated sugar on medium speed until creamy, about 2 minutes. Turn off the mixer and scrape down the bowl with a rubber spatula. Add 1 egg and beat on medium speed until blended. Add the other egg and the vanilla and beat until blended. Turn off the mixer and add the flour mixture. Mix on low speed just until blended. Add the oats and coconut and mix on low speed just until combined. Add the toasted almonds and the chocolate chips and mix just until combined. Scrape down the bowl.

Drop heaping tablespoons of the dough onto the prepared baking sheets, spacing the mounds about 1 inch apart. Bake for 7 minutes, then rotate the cookie sheets. Continue to bake until the edges of the cookies are golden brown, about 6 minutes more. Remove the cookie sheets from the oven and set them on a wire rack. Let cool for 5 minutes, then use a metal spatula to move the cookies directly to the rack. Let the cookies cool completely and serve.

# Hot Chocolate Cookies

Do you love a big mug of hot chocolate with marshmallows floating on top? Why not try it in cookie form? These chewy chocolate cookies topped with toasty marshmallows are sure to become your new favorite chocolate treat.

⌒ **MAKES ABOUT 26 COOKIES** ⌒

**1½ cups all-purpose flour**

**½ cup unsweetened cocoa powder, plus more for dusting**

**¼ cup hot chocolate mix**

**1 teaspoon baking powder**

**¼ teaspoon salt**

**3 large eggs**

**1⅔ cups sugar**

**2 teaspoons vanilla extract**

**4 tablespoons (½ stick) unsalted butter, melted and cooled slightly**

**1 bag mini marshmallows or 13 regular-size marshmallows, halved crosswise**

In a bowl, whisk together the flour, cocoa powder, hot chocolate mix, baking powder, and salt. In the bowl of an electric mixer, beat the eggs, sugar, and vanilla on high speed until light in color and thick, about 3 minutes. Add the butter and beat on medium speed until blended. Scrape down the bowl with a rubber spatula. Add the flour mixture and mix on low speed just until blended. Cover the bowl with plastic wrap and refrigerate for 1 hour.

Position 2 racks evenly in the oven and preheat to 350°F. Line 2 cookie sheets with parchment paper. Scoop up heaping tablespoonfuls of the chilled dough, roll them into balls between the palms of your hands, and place on the prepared cookie sheets, spacing them 2 inches apart.

Bake for 6 minutes, then rotate the cookie sheets. Continue to bake until the cookies are puffed and look dry, 4–6 minutes more. Let cool on a wire rack for 5 minutes, then move the cookies directly to the rack.

Once they are all baked, arrange the cookies in a single layer on one unlined cookie sheet. Position an oven rack 6 inches below the broiler and preheat the broiler. Place a few mini marshmallows on the center of each cookie (or, if using regular-size, place a marshmallow half cut-side-down on the center of each cookie). Broil until the marshmallows are gooey and golden (watch them carefully!). Let cool on a wire rack. Just before serving, put a spoonful of cocoa powder in a fine-mesh sieve and lightly dust the cookies with cocoa.

# Lemon Crinkle Cookies

These pretty cookies—a lemon lover's dream—have thin, crisp shells covered in snowy sugar. Inside is a bright burst of edible sunshine and irresistible chewiness. The dough has to chill, so make it the night before your cookie party.

*MAKES ABOUT 28 COOKIES*

**2 cups all-purpose flour**

**2 teaspoons baking powder**

**¼ tsp salt**

**½ cup (1 stick) unsalted butter, at room temperature**

**1 cup granulated sugar**

**1 tablespoon finely grated lemon zest**

**3 large eggs**

**3 tablespoons fresh lemon juice**

**1 teaspoon vanilla extract**

**½ cup powdered sugar, sifted**

 In a bowl, whisk together the flour, baking powder, and salt. In a large bowl, using an electric mixer, beat the butter, granulated sugar, and lemon zest on medium speed until creamy, about 2 minutes. Add the eggs one at a time, beating well after adding each one. Turn off the mixer and scrape down the bowl with a rubber spatula. Add the lemon juice and vanilla and beat until blended. Turn off the mixer. Add the flour mixture and mix on low speed just until blended. Cover the bowl with plastic wrap and refrigerate for at least 1 hour or up to overnight.

Position 2 racks evenly in the oven and preheat to 350°F. Line 2 cookie sheets with parchment paper. Put the powdered sugar into a shallow bowl.

Scoop up a tablespoonful of the chilled dough and roll it into a rough ball between the palms of your hands (the dough will be very sticky, so you will need to wash your hands occasionally while you are forming dough balls), then drop it into the powdered sugar and roll until completely covered. Place the balls on the prepared cookie sheets, spacing them about 2 inches apart. Press down on the dough balls to flatten them slightly.

Bake for 7 minutes, then rotate the cookie sheets. Continue to bake until the cookies are cracked and puffed and the edges are just starting to brown, about 6 minutes more. Let cool on a wire rack for 5 minutes, then use a metal spatula to move the cookies directly to the rack. Let cool completely and serve.

# Index

# weldonowen

1045 Sansome Street, San Francisco, CA 94111
www.weldonowen.com

Weldon Owen is a division of Bonnier Publishing USA

WELDON OWEN, INC.
President & Publisher  Roger Shaw
SVP, Sales & Marketing  Amy Kaneko
Finance & Operations Director  Philip Paulick

Associate Publisher  Amy Marr
Project Editor  Kim Laidlaw

Creative Director  Kelly Booth
Associate Art Director  Lisa Berman
Original Design  Alexandra Zeigler
Senior Production Designer  Rachel Lopez Metzger
Production Director  Chris Hemesath
Associate Production Director  Michelle Duggan
Imaging Manager  Don Hill

Photographer  Nicole Hill Gerulat
Food Stylists  Erin Quon, Pearl Jones
Prop Stylist  Veronica Olson
Hair & Makeup  Kathy Hill

AMERICAN GIRL *PARTIES*
Conceived and produced by Weldon Owen, Inc.
In collaboration with Williams-Sonoma, Inc.
3250 Van Ness Avenue, San Francisco, CA 94109

A WELDON OWEN PRODUCTION
Copyright © 2016 Weldon Owen, Inc.,
Williams-Sonoma, Inc., and American Girl
All rights reserved, including the right of
reproduction in whole or in part in any form.
All American Girl marks are owned by and used
under license from American Girl.

Printed and bound in the United States

First printed in 2016
10 9 8 7 6 5 4 3 2 1

Library of Congress Cataloging in Publication
data is available

ISBN 13: 978-1-68188-138-6
ISBN 10: 1-68188-138-1

ACKNOWLEDGMENTS
Weldon Owen wishes to thank the following people for their generous support to help produce this book: Erica Allen, Lisa Atwood, Maggie Broadbent, Milan Cook, Alexa Hyman, Lily Lovell, Rachel Markowitz, Alexis Mersel, Taylor Olson, Elizabeth Parson, Jennifer Paul, Tatum Quon, Alan Vance, Emely Vertiz, Tamara White, and Dawn Yanagihara

A VERY SPECIAL THANK YOU TO:
Our models: Annabelle Armstrong-Temple, Tallulah Armstrong-Temple, Krischelle Delgado, Lauren Finkelstein, Brooklyn Gorton, Harlan Groetchen, Juliet Hanks, Miranda Harvey, Hannah Hopkins, Hallie Johnson, Tatum Quon, Luke Smith, Delilah Sophia-Siegal, Terrapin Teague, Empress Toney, Colin Tuilevaka, Jr., and Naomi Wang

Our locations: Jill Bergman, The Hawkes Family, Tonya Lemone, The Sorensen Family

Our party supplies: Knot and Bow, Cranky Cakes Shop, Shop Sweet Lulu, Rice

Our clothing: Lali Kids, Tea Collection, Rubies and Gold